YOUR COMEBACK

INTERACTIVE WORKBOOK

TONY EVANS

HARVEST HOUSE PUBLISHERS
EUGENE, OREGON

All Scripture quotations are taken from the New American Standard Bible®, © 1960, 1962, 1963, 1968, 1971, 1972, 1973, 1975, 1977, 1995 by The Lockman Foundation. Used by permission. (www.Lockman.org)

Cover design by Bryce Williamson

Cover Image © Lauren Guy Photography

Your Comeback Interactive Workbook
Copyright © 2018 by Tony Evans
Published by Harvest House Publishers
Eugene, Oregon 97408
www.harvesthousepublishers.com

ISBN 978-0-7369-7289-5 (pbk.)

Printed in the United States of America

23 24 25 26 27 28 / GP-GL / 10 9 8 7 6 5 4 3

CONTENTS

MAKING THE MOST OF THIS INTERACTIVE WORKBOOK

This interactive workbook is a tool to help your group combine the video and Bible study into a dynamic growth experience. If you are the leader or facilitator of your group, take some time in advance to consider the questions in the Video Group Discussion and Group Bible Exploration portions of this guide and prepare your own personal examples to encourage discussion. To get the most out of this study, each group member should have their own copy of this *Interactive Workbook*. This will allow them to take notes during the group time and to dig deeper on their own throughout the week.

Every group session includes a video portion, so think about the logistics in advance. Will everyone be able to see the screen clearly? Make sure to set the audio at a comfortable level before the session. You don't want your group to miss anything.

With that in mind, let's preview the guide. Each lesson has six sections:

Video Teaching Notes

Several key points and quotes from the video are provided in this section, but there's also room to write down your own notes. Each video session will include real-life stories as well as teaching from Dr. Evans.

Video Group Discussion

People are likely to forget the content unless they review it right away. Many of the discussion questions have to do with remembering what they just viewed. But other questions try to connect the video to their emotions or experience. *How did you feel when they said that? Is that true in your life? Do you have the same issue?*

Group Bible Exploration

This is a Bible study, so each session is grounded in Scripture. Your group members may have different levels of faith. This is a time to open up the Bible and grow as a group or help others find their faith.

In Closing

The goal for every Bible study is to apply what you've learned. This section will highlight the main point of the lesson and challenge your group to spend some time in the coming week diving deeper into the week's theme.

On Your Own Between Sessions

This section includes additional study individuals can do to keep the content they just learned fresh in their minds throughout the week and to put it into practice.

Recommended Reading

Your group time in this video Bible study will be enhanced if everyone takes the time to read the recommended chapters in *Your Comeback* by Tony Evans. Dr. Evans's video teaching follows the book, but the book includes considerably more information and illustrations. If you are the leader, encourage your group to prepare ahead as well.

A SHIFT IN PERSPECTIVE

When you get your comeback, don't just look to God to turn your situation around. Instead, trust Him also to restore the years the locusts have stolen (Joel 2:25). That's how great God is. God is so incredibly awesome, He can not only fix what is wrong but also give you back what you have lost. That's why you should never give up hope, regardless of how long you've struggled. God can turn back the hands of time.

But before He can do that, He needs you to think different. Before God can give you your complete comeback—your double portion—He needs you to set down your pride, dignity, and rationale. God needs you to seek Him and His Word concerning your situation so He can tell you what to do. And then He wants you to obey completely.

Your Comeback, pages 18–19

Video Teaching Notes

As you watch the video, use the space below to take notes. Some key points and quotes are provided here as reminders.

Zach's Story

At a young age, Zach's father abandoned his family, leaving him to forge his own way in becoming a man. His father's absence left him wandering and alone until he met Christ and received a new identity by faith. Now God has given Zach a passion to mentor young, fatherless men and help them live positive, productive, Christ-centered lives.

Zach's story illustrates the heart of a comeback. Regardless of our past or present struggles, God is able to turn our lives around to display His glory and to empower us to minister to those in need.

Teaching 1: Tony Evans

1. What constitutes a comeback? It's more than success in life—it's a reversal from defeat to success.

2. Describe a situation in your life in which you need to bounce back.

3. Comebacks can take place after…

    sickness or injury

    financial devastation

    natural disasters

    divorce

    career setbacks

    abuse

    personal defeat in an area of sin

Quotables

- Faith is all about thinking different, about taking God at His unconventional word.
- Again and again, God thinks different.
- God always demands full faith.
- Your comeback is when God enables you to see a reversal in your circumstances.

Ursula's Story

For years, Ursula suffered sexual abuse from her adopted father…until he committed suicide. After that, she carried the guilt of feeling as though she caused his death, which led her to pursue unhealthy relationships with men. She recognized her pain but felt the need to fix it herself until God brought her to the end of herself. When she cried out to God, He changed everything.

We are often tempted to believe we are responsible for fixing what is broken in our lives. Many of us have tried to pick ourselves up by our bootstraps, but God requires a different way of thinking, one that trusts Him and follows Him wherever He calls.

Teaching 2: Tony Evans

1. Thinking different includes…

   choosing God's perspective

   stepping out in faith

   proceeding without all of the facts

   expecting good things to come out of a negative situation

2. Human wisdom includes…

   seeing the end before moving toward it

testing the outcomes first

expectations based on current realities

low risk, high gain

Video Group Discussion

1. What did you learn from Zach's and Ursula's stories? What setbacks did they face, and how did they respond? You may not be struggling with exactly the same challenges, but what do their stories teach you about facing life's difficulties?

2. We encounter a variety of setbacks in life. How can you tell whether God is setting you up for a comeback or teaching you something in the wilderness season?

3. God's instruction through the prophet to Naaman to dip seven times in the Jordan River didn't seem to make sense. What things have you felt God lead you to do that didn't appear to make sense? How have you responded?

4. How would you describe the difference between thinking with human wisdom and thinking different? Do you know people who exemplify thinking different in faith?

   a. On the continuum below, where would you put your own thinking? Circle the appropriate number.

Thinking Patterns in Everyday Activities

Human ways: *God's ways:*
money, power, and influence   *acts of obedience in faith*

1	2	3	4	5	6	7	8	9	10	11	12

b. Where do you think you were, say, ten years ago? Circle the appropriate number and then draw an arrow from the number you circled earlier to the number you just now circled. What's your trend? Are you growing and developing in this area, staying the same, or regressing?

5. "A comeback is when God intervenes in your circumstances when they desperately need to change. Whatever it is, or for however long it's been there, God is bigger than your crisis," Dr. Evans says in the video. "God is bigger than your chaos and greater than your struggle. If you will focus on Him, His Word, His promises, and His provisions, you too can have a testimony. You too can celebrate what a comeback looks like." According to this quote, what can you do to set yourself up for a comeback?

Group Bible Exploration

Read Together

"For My thoughts are not your thoughts, nor are your ways My ways," declares the LORD. "For as the heavens are higher than the earth, so are My ways higher than your ways and My thoughts than your thoughts" (Isaiah 55:8-9).

1. This verse talks about the difference between God's ways and thoughts and our own. The contrast is drastic. What can you surmise from these two verses?

2. Why would it be important for God to tell us that His thoughts are so vastly different from ours? What should our response be?

Read Together

Now Naaman, captain of the army of the king of Aram, was a great man with his master, and highly respected, because by him the LORD had given victory to Aram. The man was also a valiant warrior, but he was a leper (2 Kings 5:1).

1. What were Naaman's strengths? What were likely his past successes?

2. How might Naaman have felt about his abilities and connections—assured? Fearful? Courageous? Confident?

3. What was Naaman's setback? How did that impact his current prospects?

4. In what ways can past successes and accomplishments inhibit future growth? Is it possible to trust too much in yourself or in old ways? Why or why not?

Read Together

She said to her mistress, "I wish that my master were with the prophet who is in Samaria! Then he would cure him of his leprosy." Naaman went in and told his master, saying, "Thus and thus spoke the girl who is from the land of Israel." Then the king of Aram said, "Go now, and I will send a letter to the king of Israel." He departed and took with him ten talents of silver and six thousand shekels of gold and ten changes of clothes (2 Kings 5:3-5).

1. How did the king of Aram seek to solve Naaman's issue? How do you think Naaman felt about this approach?

2. In Naaman's day, money brought power. The king's desire to buy a healing for Naaman resembled many religious practices of that time. Does the one true God need anyone's money? In what way can money buy a comeback (if at all)?

3. While Naaman was traveling to see the prophet, how might he have felt about the idea? As you seek your personal comeback, what is the basis of your confidence?

4. This passage ends with the added information that Naaman took with him ten changes of clothes. What would that indicate about how confident both he and the king were that their money would purchase his healing? What things or spiritual rituals do you use to "negotiate" a comeback in your own life?

Read Together

Elisha sent a messenger to him, saying, "Go and wash in the Jordan seven times, and your flesh will be restored to you and you will be clean." But Naaman was furious and went away and said, "Behold, I thought, 'He will surely come out to me and stand and call on the name of the LORD his God, and wave his hand over the place and cure the leper.' Are not Abanah and Pharpar, the rivers of Damascus, better than all the waters of Israel? Could I not wash in them and be clean?" So he turned and went away in a rage (2 Kings 5:10-12).

1. What were Elisha's instructions to Naaman? And through whom did Naaman hear those instructions?

2. How did Naaman respond to hearing the instructions through a messenger? Why do you think that offended him?

3. What emotions welled up in Naaman when he was told to wash seven times in the Jordan river?

4. Have you ever been disappointed, felt slighted, or become angry when the Lord instructed you to do something? If so, take a moment to share that experience and what you learned from it.

Read Together

Then his servants came near and spoke to him and said, "My father, had the prophet told you to do some great thing, would you not have done it? How much more then, when he says to you, 'Wash, and be clean'?" So he went down and dipped himself seven times in the Jordan, according to the word of the man of God; and his flesh was restored like the flesh of a little child and he was clean (2 Kings 5:13-14).

1. What truth did Naaman's servants use to persuade him to obey? Were they successful in helping him understand that what appeared to be simple was actually a great act of faith?

2. How can we shift our own perspectives to view faith acts as important steps even when the acts themselves may seem insignificant?

3. What did you learn from Naaman's eventual obedience? In what way can you apply this to a personal situation you are facing?

In Closing

As you end the study today, pray together for openness. Open yourselves to God's ability and desire to shift your thinking toward His perspective. Ask Him for the courage to be open to His leading—even if He asks you to take some surprising next steps!

Before session two, complete the following "On Your Own Between Sessions." At the beginning of the next session, consider sharing what you learned.

On Your Own Between Sessions

1. In the story we studied from 2 Kings 5, we saw two ways to try to reverse a setback. The first way was through human wisdom, which involved money, power, and influence. The second way was through God's wisdom, which includes an action of obedience in faith. Which approach do you tend to use in your everyday decisions?

   The truth is, the way we act or react in our everyday activities will often affect the way we respond to larger challenges. Establishing a pattern of faith in your everyday thinking is critical to living a life that will set you up for a comeback.

2. Read the story of Abraham and Isaac in Genesis 22:1-14. If you're used to a particular translation, mix it up a bit by going with a new one, just to get fresh eyes on the story. This is a familiar Bible lesson—you probably know what happens—but let's pay special attention to what happens when Abraham acts in in faith. List some of the things God asked Abraham to do, and then list what the normal human response would be.

God's Request	Human Wisdom

3. No one following human wisdom would have hiked up the mountain to sacrifice his or her heir, through whom the promised blessing would come. Human wisdom would encourage a helicopter parent to shield the son from danger. But Abraham feared God more than he trusted himself. And his actions of obedience led to great favor.

How can Abraham's obedience help us to understand just how different God really does think? Does anything scare God? Why or why not? How can we incorporate God's sovereignty into our own way of thinking?

4. What emotions did Abraham and Naaman have to experience in order to carry out such far-reaching actions? What convictions did they need?

5. List some of the emotions and convictions that prompt us to do things our way. Then contrast them with reasons to do things God's way.

Reasons to Do What We Want and Know	Reasons to Do What God Says

6. Life Experiment: Think Different Day

Pick a day this week to experiment with thinking different. Shortly after you wake up, talk with God, letting Him know that you desire to align all your thoughts and actions (however minor) with Him. Tell him you choose to follow His direction and guidance that day. Then, as you go through the day, keep the communication channel with God open.

This might mean praying, reading, paying attention to the needs around you, paying attention to how you spend your time, and so on. Let God into every moment of your day and seek to discern His voice.

7. Life Experiment Follow-Up

After trying the Think Different Day experiment, talk about it with someone. Was it good, weird, hard, instructive, frustrating, life-changing, pointless...? Write some of your thoughts here, and consider talking about it when you gather for the next session of *Your Comeback*.

Recommended Reading

In preparation for session two, read chapters 2 and 3 of *Your Comeback*. To review the material from session one, read chapter 1.

A HEART OF PARTICIPATION

Everyone loves a comeback. The masses cheer for the underdog in sports just so they can get the emotional high of watching a comeback. We tear up and applaud for those who have overcome seemingly insurmountable health issues. When a lost pet is found and returned home, as was the case of one dog stranded at sea after a tsunami in Japan, millions of people tune in to watch their meaningful reunion on social media for years to come.

Something innate within us longs to see or experience a comeback. When all looked lost, we thrill to discover that it's not over after all. That things can turn around, even on a dime, and point us in the right direction...

Comebacks inspire us because they help us believe that whatever we might be facing—whether it's a financial setback, a health challenge, a relational breakup, or simply discouragement—we too can rise once again to the dawn of a new day. If it turned around for them, it can turn around for us. It helps us believe that where we are today does not have to determine where we will be tomorrow. Comebacks give us hope, and hope is the very thing that makes our hearts beat strong.

Your Comeback, pages 24–25

Video Teaching Notes

As you watch the video, use the space below to take notes. Some key points and quotes are provided here as reminders.

Cameron's Story

As a child, Cameron dreamed of becoming a pilot. On his way to what appeared to be a successful career in aviation, he broke his back in a water skiing accident, which placed him on a five-year waiting period before he could be considered for a pilot's license. Despite his circumstances, Cameron has continued to trust God's sovereignty and works in aviation management, where he embraces regular opportunities to share his faith.

Life does not always work out according to our plans, but God is sovereign nonetheless. Sometimes He takes us on unusual paths, but when we are faithful to obey, our intimacy with Him grows, and we are able to bless others as a result.

Teaching 1: Tony Evans

1. Disappointments come in all areas of life.

2. Trusting Jesus when He doesn't seem to be making sense is one way to live with great expectations. Are you willing to trust Jesus the way Peter did when Jesus told him to put his net on the other side of the boat?

Quotables

- God is the Architect of the great reversal. He helped a scrawny boy with five stones to defeat a nine-foot giant.
- Comebacks are God's specialty. They bring Him glory.
- God wants to give you a comeback for several reasons:

to show you who He is

to show you who you are

to show you your purpose

to show you to follow Him

- God wants to bless you so you will have more time for Him.

Bonnie's Story

With a stable career, a loving husband, and the promise of a second child, Bonnie had it all—until she received a phone call informing her that her husband had been killed in a car accident. Her life changed dramatically, but God faithfully provided for her, and now she has remarried and ministers the hope of the gospel to widows.

It would have been easy for Bonnie to stay down after losing her husband, but she chose to trust God despite her fear and confusion. Through that process, she watched God provide for her needs and give her opportunities to use her experience as a way of helping others embrace hope in their loss.

Teaching 2: Tony Evans

1. Life has a way of knocking us down, but faith is a participatory act.

2. God invites us to play a part in the work He is doing in us and through us. This means that the Christian life can never become one of passive inactivity.

3. God wants us to devote our hearts to Him entirely. He sometimes calls us to unusual forms of obedience so we will come to desire Him more than we desire anything else.

4. The way of faith is to follow Him no matter how strange the path may seem.

Video Group Discussion

1. In Cameron's story, we saw how quickly things can change on the path to our dreams. Disappointments can come out of the blue and delay us from reaching our goals and aspirations. Have you ever experienced a shift on your path that caused an unexpected delay? Or have you witnessed this in someone's life? What was the most beneficial way of responding? What responses make things worse?

2. Bonnie was eventually able to help others find hope after loss. Is God using something in your life to enable you to comfort or encourage others? Are you willing to use the pain of the past to help others through their own pain?

3. The video included the story of Peter fishing all night long and having nothing to show for it. Dr. Evans mentioned that Peter must have felt weary and discouraged. When we feel that way—when life is pressing in on us, when our expectations are not met, when our finances are low, when our relationships are stressed—being willing to try something new is harder than ever. Yet Peter obeyed and rowed out to the deep water to fish again. In what way do your own emotions prevent you from going on or trying something again in the face of huge disappointments? Do you have a strategy for overcoming negative emotions? If so, what is it?

4. How did track star Heather Dorniden respond after she fell down during her race? What principles can you learn from her example?

5. Did Heather let her negative emotions cloud her decision to keep going?

6. Dr. Evans said in the video, "Sometimes God will keep us in a place that doesn't look like it's going anywhere because He is after something much bigger than answered prayer." Explain what you think this statement means. How does it apply to Hannah's situation of infertility?

   a. How does Dr. Evans's statement above apply to a situation you are facing now or one you have faced in the past?

   b. Based on Hannah's and Joseph's biblical examples, what are some good ways to respond to what seem like unmet needs or unanswered prayer?

Group Bible Exploration

Read Together

When He had finished speaking, He said to Simon, "Put out into the deep water and let down your nets for a catch." Simon answered and said, "Master, we worked hard all night and caught nothing, but I will do as You say and let down the nets." When they had done this, they enclosed a great quantity of fish, and their nets began to break; so they signaled to their partners in the other boat for them to come and help them. And they came and filled both of the boats, so that they began to sink. But when Simon Peter saw that, he fell down at Jesus' feet, saying, "Go away from me Lord, for I am a sinful man!" For amazement had seized him and all his companions because of the catch of fish which they had taken (Luke 5:4-9).

1. In your own words, what is the main point of this story?

2. Why do you think Peter fell down and asked Jesus to go away? Would that have been your response? Why or why not?

3. Let's connect the principles from this story to what we've looked at so far in comebacks. Do people usually have to hit rock bottom (that is, experience extreme disappointment, failure, emptiness, or similar things) before coming back? Do you tend to deny failures or disappointments in your life, or are you open to acknowledging and embracing them as part of life?

4. Did Jesus's instructions to put the nets out in the deep water make sense to the fishermen? Have you ever felt that God was directing you to do something that didn't make sense to you? What do you tend to do when God asks you to do something that seems to be illogical?

Read Together

We walk by faith, not by sight (2 Corinthians 5:7).

Now to Him who is able to do far more abundantly beyond all that we ask or think, according to the power that works within us...(Ephesians 3:20).

1. Can you trace a connection between these two verses? If so, what is it?

> Peter got to witness the comeback only after he did something contrary to his own instincts, something that even seemed ridiculous.
>
> Going from an empty boat to a net-breaking catch of fish is an emotional comeback, a career comeback, a financial comeback, and a spiritual comeback. But Peter had to adjust his will to God's will in order to get there. He had to move before he realized that Jesus knew exactly where those fish were all along (*Your Comeback*, page 32).

2. In what way do the two Scriptures above support this quote?

3. Have you ever asked God to increase your faith? What was the result?

4. Are you willing to make a habit of asking God to continually increase your faith? Why or why not?

5. What might be the result if you did?

Read Together

Barnabas and Saul returned from Jerusalem when they had fulfilled their mission, taking along with them John, who was also called Mark (Acts 12:25).

When they reached Salamis, they began to proclaim the word of God in the synagogues of the Jews; and they also had John as their helper (Acts 13:5).

Now Paul and his companions put out to sea from Paphos and came to Perga in Pamphylia; but John left them and returned to Jerusalem (Acts 13:13).

Paul kept insisting that they should not take him along who had deserted them in Pamphylia and had not gone with them to the work. And there occurred such a sharp disagreement that they separated from one another, and Barnabas took Mark with him and sailed away to Cyprus. But Paul chose Silas and left, being committed by the brethren to the grace of the Lord (Acts 15:38-40).

1. Describe John Mark's situation as a missionary. What was his setback? Why do you think he may have abandoned his role?

2. How difficult is it to come back from a personal, moral failure? How did Mark's failure affect Paul's and Barnabas's confidence in him?

3. Acts 4:36 explains that Barnabas is an encourager. In what way is giving someone a second chance a form of encouragement?

4. If you can, describe a time in your own life when you failed, but others encouraged you. (If that is too difficult, describe someone else's similar experience without revealing their identity.) How did the encouragement—discovering that others still believed in you—help you experience a comeback? Who can you give that encouragement to this week?

Read Together

I have received everything in full and have an abundance; I am amply supplied, having received from Epaphroditus what you have sent, a fragrant aroma, an acceptable sacrifice, well-pleasing to God. And my God will supply all your needs according to His riches in glory in Christ Jesus. Now to our God and Father be the glory forever and ever. Amen (Philippians 4:18-20).

1. What progression do you see in these three verses?

2. What is the connection between (1) the Philippians' supplying Paul's needs, and (2) God supplying the Philippians' needs?

3. To what end were these provisions made (verse 20)?

4. How important is the connection between God's glory and your comeback?

Read Together

Give, and it will be given to you. They will pour into your lap a good measure—pressed down, shaken together, and running over. For by your standard of measure it will be measured to you in return (Luke 6:38).

1. Dr. Evans talked about the importance of giving away the same thing (the "it") we hope to receive. For example, if you are in a financial setback, then give graciously to someone else. Or if you are experiencing relational barrenness, then look for a lonely person to encourage, such as a shut-in. In what way did this impact your thinking on how to more actively participate in your own comeback?

2. Have you given something away and then watched God give even more of "it" back to you?

3. Can you share a biblical example of someone receiving what they needed only after they gave it away?

In Closing

As you end today's study, pray together for resilience. Perhaps some in the group can share their personal setbacks—what they are struggling to overcome or come back from. Ask God for insight, for discernment, and for a daily dose of strength.

Before session three, complete the "On Your Own Between Sessions" section below. You might want to review that section at the beginning of session three.

On Your Own Between Sessions

1. Chapter 2 in *Your Comeback* mentioned two specific signs of a comeback:

   • God allows all of your efforts to be unsuccessful.

   • God then asks you to do something that doesn't make sense.

   a. Is there an area in your life where you feel that God has allowed all your efforts to be unsuccessful? Or can you identify a pattern of Him blocking advancement in your life or someone else's life?

   b. Is it possible that this blockage is actually setting the stage for a comeback? Why or why not?

   c. Why do you think God often uses these two signs when initiating divine reversals, or comebacks, in people's lives?

2. Read 1 Samuel 2:21. How many children did Hannah ultimately have?

    a. Hannah was willing to give to God. What part did this play in God's provision to her?

    b. What might God want you to give to Him for His glory?

    c. What hesitations do you feel when you think about giving something or someone back to God?

3. In the video, Dr. Evans said,

    Many people—in fact, most people—know what it is to fall. To hit the ground, running, whether you tripped over your own feet or whether you've tripped over the feet of someone else. You've become disappointed that you are now down for what appears the count. Ah, but like Heather, God is able to take things that don't look like they could ever work out, turn them around, and still bring you to victory—even though it looks like you lost time, strength, and opportunity.

    a. In what ways has God renewed your strength and created opportunities when you felt they were lost?

    b. Take some time now to think and pray, asking God to bring about a great reversal in your situation or setback. Ask Him to give you the faith to get back up, keep going, and live life with energy, passion, and great expectations.

c. Whatever you are facing, do you believe God is able to turn it around and use it for good? Why or why not?

4. On your own or with your spouse or a trusted friend, think of ways you can seek God to discern His will and direction for the steps of faith He wants you to take. As you pray and discuss this, write down some things you can do to demonstrate your confidence that God is able to give you a comeback in your area of need. Use the chart below if it helps. We've provided one example to get you started.

Need	Faith Steps	Give It to Others	Give It to God
1. Relational closeness with someone.	1. Offer relational closeness to others.	1. Visit a shut-in once a week.	1. When God provides a new relationship, find ways to serve Him in it.

a. As you look back over the chart, can you see any patterns in what you feel God is leading you to do?

b. To avoid feeling overwhelmed, write down one or two small but important steps God might be asking you to take.

5. Life Experiment: Participating in Your Comeback

a. *Identify* one area in your life where you need a comeback. How do you normally react to the situation?

b. *Consider* some better ways for you to respond. What steps could you take?

c. *Evaluate* how to proceed. You don't need to do something just because it doesn't make sense. Ask God to confirm what He is asking you to do. He can speak to you in your heart, through His Word, and through trustworthy believers.

d. *Choose* what you will do when an opportunity comes along this week.

e. *Learn* from the process. Did your circumstances change after you stepped out in faith? Did you experience God's peace when you took action? Can you establish these new patterns of thinking and acting in your life?

Recommended Reading

In preparation for session three, read chapters 4 and 5 of *Your Comeback*.

KEEP MOVING, KEEP PRAYING

When you are in a situation that you feel is holding you hostage, you often have to reach that point of desperation before you stop being willing to settle for your circumstances. It may be bad, but you're alive. It may be hopeless, but you're making it each day. Tragically, many people don't get ahead or discover their comeback because they have decided to settle where they are.

Your Comeback, page 71

Video Teaching Notes

As you watch the video, use the space below to take notes. Some key points and quotes are provided here as reminders.

Alex and Ava's Story

In the middle of a pickup game of basketball, Alex went into cardiac arrest. Doctors feared the lack of oxygen to his brain would lead to irreparable damage. Claiming the promises of God, Ava prayed fearlessly for her husband, who awoke without brain damage. Alex and Ava are now firmly convinced of the power of prayer.

We all face times that tempt us to give up hope, but we serve a God who is able to reverse what appears irreversible. Our sovereign God can do the impossible, just as He did with Alex and Ava.

Teaching 1: Tony Evans

1. We have all faced circumstances that tempt us to give up hope for a better future. But we know that the God of the universe can reverse even the situations that seem irreversible.

2. Rather than settle for our current situation, we must believe God for a better day and continue moving forward.

Quotables

- When things appear to be getting consistently worse rather than better, your emotions and will are tested.
- The power of God's name is connected to the content of His character.
- Sometimes we think we can get away with things no one sees, but God sees.
- "Irreversible" can lead to the deepest despair. "Irreversible" knows no cure.
- Except God.
- God knows how to bring about a comeback even in an irreversible situation.

Monica's Story

When Monica was in high school, her family opened their home to a friend from church who was in a difficult time. But the friend sexually assaulted Monica. Afterward, Monica felt alone, fell into a deep depression, and began to shut people out. Yet God pursued her in her pain and delivered her from hopelessness to hope in Christ.

Now Monica is no longer trapped by her past. Instead, she uses her experiences to minister to women who have been rescued from prostitution and sex trafficking.

Regardless of what we have been through, God can redeem us from our past. He is the one who defines us, which means we can trust Him in every crisis of life.

Teaching 2: Tony Evans

1. No one's life is free of crisis.

2. During His earthly life, Jesus promised His followers that trials would come. But He also promised to walk with them through those trials. That promise still holds true for us today.

3. When we face a crisis, we should trust in the sufficiency of Christ rather than our own abilities.

Video Group Discussion

1. Dr. Evans made some pretty strong statements in the video, including this one:

   When you become a minister with a ministry coming out of your misery, you will discover that the irreversible can be made reversible by an all-powerful God to bring about your comeback.

   a. Do you agree with this? Why or why not?

   b. If this is true, what are the implications for your life?

   c. How can this help you to embrace your pain and use what you have learned to help others in their own comeback?

2. Everything around Alex and Ava looked bleak, but Ava did not give up. Instead, she kept calling on God in the midst of the darkness.

a. In what way does their testimony bring you encouragement?

b. Would you like to adopt their approach to prayer and tragedy? What would that look like for you?

3. What do you think Dr. Evans meant when he said the lepers became "a vehicle for blessing to others"?

a. Have you ever experienced this yourself? What was the situation?

b. How can you become even more of a vehicle for blessing to others?

4. Dr. Evans mentioned in his teaching that "God will sometimes put you on the canvas— take away all of your props—so that it's just you and Him." Do you agree with this? Why or why not?

a. Why would God want to do something like that?

    b. Have you ever seen God provide a way where there was no way, or reverse a seemingly impossible situation? If you have, what does that tell you about His ability to provide a comeback for you?

5. Dr. Evans mentions three things King Jehoshaphat does in his prayer:

- He begins by affirming how big and capable God is. He magnifies God's strengths and reminds himself and his citizens of God's abilities.
- He then spends time praising God for His strength, His power, and more.
- Then he presents his request to God.

    a. Consider something you are struggling with right now. Take some time to jot down three to five attributes of God.

    b. Next, write statements of praise to God for those each of those attributes.

    c. Finally, write your requests for God to display those attributes in your situation.

Group Bible Exploration

Read Together

As each one has received a special gift, employ it in serving one another as good stewards of the manifold grace of God. Whoever speaks, is to do so as one who is speaking the utterances of God; whoever serves is to do so as one who is serving by the strength which God supplies; so that in all things God may be glorified through Jesus Christ, to whom belongs the glory and dominion forever and ever. Amen (1 Peter 4:10-11).

Slaves, in all things obey those who are your masters on earth, not with external service, as those who merely please men, but with sincerity of heart, fearing the Lord. Whatever you do, do your work heartily, as for the Lord rather than for men, knowing that from the Lord you will receive the reward of the inheritance. It is the Lord Christ whom you serve (Colossians 3:22-24).

1. Based on these passages, what should be your motivation for serving God?

2. You're not a slave, so how does Colossians 3:22-24 apply to you?

3. In what way is serving others connected to your comeback?

Read Together

"The leprosy of Naaman shall cling to you [Gehazi] and to your descendants forever." So he went out from his presence a leper as white as snow (2 Kings 5:27).

Now the king was talking with Gehazi, the servant of the man of God, saying, "Please relate to me all the great things that Elisha has done" (2 Kings 8:4).

1. At first glance, these verses seem to be referring to two completely different people. Lepers were "unclean" in biblical days, and no leper would be granted an audience with the king. Yet these passages refer to the same man. How significant is Gehazi's healing from leprosy?

2. Most people would say being healed from leprosy is impossible. Yet God is the God of the impossible. God does some of His best work in the dark. What is the spiritual reversal that happened to Gehazi (look closely at 2 King 5:27)?

3. Is it reasonable for us to believe God would reverse the negative consequences of our own sin? Why or why not?

Read Together

Your iniquities have made a separation between you and your God, and your sins have hidden His face from you so that He does not hear (Isaiah 59:2).

1. What does sin do to our relationship with God?

2. In what way can unconfessed sin hinder you from achieving your comeback?

Read Together

Jehoshaphat the king of Judah returned in safety to his house in Jerusalem. Jehu the son of Hanani the seer went out to meet him and said to King Jehoshaphat, "Should you help the wicked and love those who hate the LORD and so bring wrath on yourself from the LORD? But there is some good in you, for you have removed the Asheroth from the land and you have set your heart to seek God" (2 Chronicles 19:1-3).

1. When someone joins with the wicked for personal gain, how can that person receive help from the Lord? What does this say about God's ability to forgive us when we repent?

2. What's the difference between repentance and regret?

3. Is there anything in your life for which you need to repent? If so, note it in the space below and write a short prayer, asking God to help you make the change. If you are not yet ready to make this step, will you take the time to ask God to help you make that choice?

Read Together

The LORD said to Gideon, "The people who are with you are too many for Me to give Midian into their hands, for Israel would become boastful, saying, 'My own power has delivered me.' Now therefore come, proclaim in the hearing of the people, saying, 'Whoever is afraid and trembling, let him return and depart from Mount Gilead.'" So 22,000 people returned, but 10,000 remained.

Then the LORD said to Gideon, "The people are still too many; bring them down to the water and I will test them for you there. Therefore it shall be that he of whom I say to you, 'This one shall go with you,' he shall go with you; but everyone of whom I say to you, 'This one shall not go with you,' he shall not go." So he brought the people down to the water. And the LORD said to Gideon, "You shall separate everyone who laps the water with his tongue as a dog laps, as well as everyone who kneels to drink." Now the number of those who lapped, putting their hand to their mouth, was 300 men; but all the rest of the people kneeled to drink water. The LORD said to Gideon, "I will deliver you with the 300 men who lapped and will give the Midianites into your hands; so let all the other people go, each man to his home." So the 300 men took the people's provisions and their trumpets into their hands. And Gideon sent all the other men of Israel, each to his tent, but retained the 300 men; and the camp of Midian was below him in the valley (Judges 7:2-8).

1. As we have learned in our study, God brings Himself glory by reversing the irreversible. Why do you think He asked Gideon to shrink his army from 32,000 men to 300?

2. Gideon and his 300 men went on to win the battle. What do you think the victorious warriors would say if someone asked them who achieved the victory?

3. In what area of your own life might you be trying to achieve a victory or comeback by human means and methods?

   a. Could you be getting in God's way by trying to do it yourself? How might you lean on God more and lean on yourself less?

   b. Are you willing to do this? Why or why not?

In Closing

As you close your time together, encourage each other to be authentic with God. Honesty in our struggles and failures opens our hearts so true repentance can occur. Also, when we examine the ways we tend to rely on conventional wisdom and our own tools, we discover how we may be getting in the way of our comebacks.

Consider these words from Dr. Evans as you wrap up this session together:

Never allow the embarrassment of your past sin to hold you hostage to a life of wandering and regret. God is after one thing—a change of heart and character in you. He can restore you, redeem you, heal you, and even promote you if you will say, "God, reveal the flaw in my character that has caused me to make these sinful choices, and correct me so I can become who You want me to be."

God is not in a hurry. He will wait if you do not wish to grow. But if you are tired of living under the circumstances of a failed and painful existence—in any area of your life—then give God the right and permission to develop your character. If you are tired of living outside the camp, outside of God's blessings of goodness and power, invite God to show you where you have failed in the past and how you can grow in the present. Not every trial or problem is a result of our sin, but many are. If this is the case in your life, take heart; God can reverse your situation when you are willing to let Him grow you in the area where you need to grow most (*Your Comeback*, pages 77–78).

Before session four, complete the "On Your Own Between Sessions" section below. You might want to review that section at the beginning of session four.

On Your Own Between Sessions

1. Read 1 Samuel 17. This is a classic example of God reversing the irreversible. The Israelites faced certain death. No one in the entire nation was equipped to go up against Goliath. It was an unfair battle. But David chose to go despite the opposition and uneven odds.

   a. What gave David courage to fight Goliath?

   b. In what way did God honor David's courage?

   c. List some of David's character qualities. Which ones can you seek to strengthen in your own life?

Feelings always follow circumstances. They react. That's why, when you're in the midst of a crisis, you need to remind yourself what is true and real about God— that He rules over all. He rules over your finances, your career, your relationships, your children, your health, and your emotions (*Your Comeback*, page 90).

2. In what ways can our feelings deceive us? Are feelings always based on truth?

3. Can you always trust your feelings to guide you well?

4. List five truths about God to remember when you are full of anxiety, worry, doubt, regret, or hopelessness.

    a.

    b.

    c.

    d.

    e.

5. Meditation: God Is Able

    Take some quiet time this week to reflect on God's rulership over all. Consider the heavens and the earth. Consider the creation and how He holds everything together. Think about the complexity of the human body, or even just the human eye. Spend some time researching online how things grow, how the body functions, or how the weather patterns change. Whatever aspect of creation you choose to think about, you will find an intricacy that goes beyond our understanding.

    After you've allowed yourself to consider God's sovereign control, power, creativity, and ingenuity, apply those attributes of God to the issues you are facing right now. Is anything too difficult for God? Can you trust Him? Is He able?

    Let God speak these truths deep into your heart this week.

6. Read 2 Chronicles 20:20: "Put your trust in the Lord your God and you will be established." What does this mean?

a. How can you go about trusting in God in your mind? In your heart? In your actions?

b. Does trust in God have to be demonstrated in your actions?

c. When you sit in your favorite chair, you don't think twice—you trust it to hold you. How do you think God feels when we wonder whether He will care for us or grant us the victory we are seeking Him for?

d. What does worry reveal about faith and trust?

7. Life Experiment: Praise Versus Panic

This week, be intentional about choosing praise as your go-to response to things that normally make you panic.

Spend some time meditating on this decision each day so that it is at the forefront of your mind. You may want to write some little notes to put on your mirror, in the car, beside your bed, or at work. Choose a simple reminder, such as "Praise, don't panic."

By continually thinking about praising God (and actually doing it!), you will more naturally respond with praise when something chaotic or stressful happens. Don't wait until you are in the midst of a crisis to consider what to do. Plan to praise. Set yourself up to praise.

Practice praise. Make praise a regular part of your life. Then, when difficulties arise, this automatic response will help to usher in your comeback.

Recommended Reading

In preparation for session four, read chapters 6 and 7 of *Your Comeback*.

CHARACTER FORMATION

Many of us ask to know God's will by praying, "Lord, lead me." But God will not lead you into His unrevealed will until He knows you're doing something with His revealed will—His Word. He will lead you through what is unclear once you are doing what is very clear.

Some of our prayers for direction go unanswered because God sees we are not doing anything with what we already know. We must make plans according to God's Word, but then we must hand our plans over to God for His adjustment and correction, for our sanctification and growth toward Christlikeness. God will turn your plan into His plan as you build your life on His Word.

When we apply God's wisdom to our lives and live in accordance with what He has spelled out in Scripture, then we are in line for a comeback. Wisdom lets us experience God's will, because wisdom is the application of God's Word to the practical issues of life.

Your Comeback, pages 131–132

Video Teaching Notes

As you watch the video, use the space below to take notes. Some key points and quotes are provided here as reminders.

Ryan's Story

After years of training, Ryan was drafted to play major league soccer. Not long after moving, he was hit by a car and broke three bones in his neck, jeopardizing his career. In the middle of his doubts, Ryan chose to trust that God works all things together for the good of those who love Him. God has healed Ryan, who is now playing professional soccer and sharing the gospel with his teammates.

We all face trials in life, and Scripture reveals that God allows them for a purpose. As Christians, we must grow in our ability to endure, which is something we do by embracing God's promises the way Ryan did after his accident.

Teaching 1: Tony Evans

1. Trials are rarely pleasant, but God allows them for a reason.

2. Trials serve to mature our character by revealing what we truly believe.

3. Endurance is an important part of walking faithfully in a relationship with Christ during trials.

Quotables

- The double-minded person is the split-personality Christian.
- Your situation may be God's test in your life to take you to the next level of spiritual maturity.
- If your life is going to take off—if you are going to get your comeback—you have to go to God. You have to connect with God and access the wisdom only He provides.
- Even a little bit of worldly wisdom mixed with God's wisdom spells spiritual death.

Becca's Story

When Becca moved to San Francisco to pursue a career in acting, she became fearful of sharing her faith because of what her peers might think. She valued her career above her convictions...until God showed her the need to live what she claimed to believe. By God's grace, Becca has now grown in her courage to speak with those around her about the hope of Jesus Christ.

There are two ways of living—the world's way and God's way. It's easy to rationalize certain choices by calling them wise, just as Becca did to ensure the success of her career. But doing so means putting God on the back burner. We need to make sure that the wisdom we follow is in line with the Word of God.

Teaching 2: Tony Evans

1. There are two kinds of wisdom in this life:

   - The world's wisdom
   - The wisdom of God

2. One leads to death; the other leads to life.

3. Our choices reflect what kind of wisdom we depend on in life, so we need to be intentional about creating habits that cultivate godly wisdom.

Video Group Discussion

1. In the video, we met Ryan, who was on the path to playing professional soccer when he got hit by a car. Ryan faced an uphill battle simply to regain his strength and coordination. Most of the people around him thought he couldn't possibly fulfill his dream of playing professional soccer. But Ryan chose to face his trial with resilience, and he came back from the trial stronger than ever.

   a. In what ways can God use trials to develop our character?

   b. Can a person "waste" a trial or challenge by responding immaturely? Why or why not?

2. We also met Becca, who chose to rely on her own wisdom rather than God's when she started pursuing her acting career. We often call worldly wisdom "common sense."

   a. Why is it important to run your commonsense decisions through the grid of God's Word?

   b. Have you ever downplayed or hidden your faith because you feared the repercussions? What happened?

3. In the video, Dr. Evans mentions biblical examples of people who suffered difficult trials. The first was Joseph, who was thrown in a pit, sold as a slave, and unjustly imprisoned. Next Dr. Evans reminded us of Shadrach, Meshach, and Abednego, who were thrown into a fiery furnace. In what ways did God alleviate their suffering even while allowing the trial to continue?

a. Is God required to schedule our comeback according to our timetable? What are some reasons He might delay?

b. List three things you have learned from trials in your life.

4. In the video, we were challenged to ask God to show us the purpose for the pain in the midst of a trial. Let's take a few minutes now to ask this question. Spend some time in group prayer. Without going into the details of your personal trials, ask God to reveal His purpose to anyone in your group who is facing a trial at this time. Be sure to end the time of prayer thanking Him in advance for the wisdom He will reveal (James 1:5).

5. In the video, Dr. Evans defined trials this way: "Trials are negative circumstances that God either causes or allows to develop you to the next spiritual level."

a. What is the difference between God causing a trial and God allowing a trial?

b. Do you think God would ever put on someone more than they can bear? Why or why not?

Group Bible Exploration

Read Together

We do not want you to be unaware, brethren, of our affliction which came to us in Asia, that we were burdened excessively, beyond our strength, so that we despaired even of life; indeed, we had the sentence of death within ourselves so that we would not trust in ourselves, but in God who raises the dead (2 Corinthians 1:8-9).

1. Did God burden Paul with more than he could bear?

2. Why did God allow such a severe trial in Paul's life?

3. Are certain lessons easier to learn when we have reached a point of despair? Explain your answer. If you answered yes, what are a few lessons that you think are learned best after we have hit bottom?

> Trials also test our heart and reveal what is there. Without being tested, we wouldn't know where we are weak and need to fortify ourselves. We wouldn't know what impurities need to be removed from our lives if the fire of trials didn't reveal them. Trials are designed to validate in experience what you declare that you believe. Trials bring you to the point where your faith stands the test, no matter how hot the fire (*Your Comeback*, page 106).

4. Have your trials revealed anything in your own life that you were surprised to discover? If so, what?

Read Together

[You] are protected by the power of God through faith for a salvation ready to be revealed in the last time. In this you greatly rejoice, even though now for a little while, if necessary, you have been distressed by various trials, so that the proof of your faith, being more precious than gold which is perishable, even though tested by fire, may be found to result in praise and glory and honor at the revelation of Jesus Christ (1 Peter 1:5-7).

1. What is the difference between God protecting us for salvation and God allowing trials in our lives?

2. According to this passage, what result are trials intended to bring?

3. What can we do to bring the trial to an end quickly?

4. In the book, Dr. Evans compared trials to exams in school. If a student fails the exam, there is a retest. Does this comparison motivate you to "pass" your trials the first time? Why or why not?

Read Together

James, a bond-servant of God and of the Lord Jesus Christ,

To the twelve tribes who are dispersed abroad: Greetings.

Consider it all joy, my brethren, when you encounter various trials, knowing that the testing of your faith produces endurance. And let endurance have its perfect result, so that you may be perfect and complete, lacking in nothing (James 1:1-4).

1. The Greek words translated "endurance" mean "to remain under." In this context, what does it mean to you to "remain under" something?

2. What are some things we do or say that indicate we are not "remaining under" or "enduring" well?

3. James tells us that enduring trials well leads to a "perfect result." Describe what you believe that perfect result is.

4. Do you ever feel like giving up during a trial? If so, what motivates you to continue enduring well?

Read Together

Remember Jesus Christ, risen from the dead, descendant of David, according to my gospel, for which I suffer hardship even to imprisonment as a criminal; but the word of God is not imprisoned. For this reason I endure all things for the sake of those who are chosen, so that they also may obtain the salvation which is in Christ Jesus and with it eternal glory. It is a trustworthy statement:

> For if we died with Him, we will also live with Him;
> If we endure, we will also reign with Him;
> If we deny Him, He also will deny us;
> If we are faithless, He remains faithful, for He cannot deny Himself
> (2 Timothy 2:8-13).

1. Why do you think Paul valued suffering and enduring so much?

2. What do you think Paul means when he says, "If we endure, we will also reign" with Christ?

3. Could a lack of endurance possibly delay a comeback? Why or why not?

Read Together

The fear of the LORD is the beginning of wisdom,
And the knowledge of the Holy One is understanding (Proverbs 9:10).

1. Where do you go to get wisdom to help you through the trials and setbacks of life?

2. What does it mean (in your practical, everyday choices) to fear the Lord?

3. During difficult seasons in life, how often do you base your decisions on the fear of the Lord? If it is not as often as you like, commit yourself to pray, asking God to help you do that more often.

In Closing

As you end this session today, spend some time considering the importance of enduring trials and challenges with wisdom. By dignifying your difficulties, you can open the pathway for

God to move and provide your comeback sooner rather than later. Set your mind on God so that when pain clouds your emotions, your thoughts will guided by His wisdom.

Before session five, complete the "On Your Own Between Sessions" section below. You might want to review that section at the beginning of session five.

On Your Own Between Sessions

1. Colossians 2:3 tells us that in Christ "are hidden all the treasures of wisdom and knowledge." Think about your abiding relationship with Christ. As you grow closer to Him, you will experience more of His wisdom and knowledge. What three things can you do this week to abide more fully in Christ?

   1.

   2.

   3.

2. Life Experiment: Encourage Others

   One way to discover how to get through a trial with wisdom is to encourage others as they walk through their own setbacks and challenges.

   This week, think of someone who is struggling with something they have shared publicly—a health issue, a family breakdown, a career crisis, loneliness, or any other difficulty. If you cannot think of anyone, ask your small group leader or pastor if someone in your church is currently facing a critical need.

   Now, pray for wisdom to know how you can personally encourage this person all week long. Do not limit it to one thing. Think of multiple ways to bring about practical helps and encouragement. As you do, note what seems to help the most. Be sure to listen to any feedback you receive. As you invest in others, you will also discover something about yourself and know better how to face trials in your own life.

3. James 3:17 lists seven characteristics of wisdom: "The wisdom from above is first pure, then peaceable, gentle, reasonable, full of mercy and good fruits, unwavering, without hypocrisy." Take some time to consider what each of these qualities would look like in your own life. Where might they be lacking? Make notes beside each quality where you can improve. Think of ways you can better express this quality to others in your words and actions.

   a. Pure

   b. Peaceable

    c. Gentle

    d. Reasonable

    e. Full of mercy and good fruits

    f. Unwavering

    g. Without hypocrisy

4. Meditation: Wisdom

What have you been complaining about lately? What have you been troubled by? Would the qualities we just considered—the fruits of the wisdom from above—bring peace and stability to any areas of your life?

Take some time to mull over this, to pray, to feel, to be convicted, and to let the attributes found in wisdom begin to resonate more fully in you. Let the Holy Spirit guide your emotions. Ask, "How would my days and hours be different?" What would happen to your work life and home life if you let the abiding presence of Christ's wisdom infiltrate all of your conversations, decisions, and actions?

1. Read 2 Timothy 2:23-24. List four qualities God desires in His disciples.

    1.

    2.

    3.

    4.

2. How can these qualities strengthen you to endure trials with wisdom and experience a comeback more quickly?

Recommended Reading

In preparation for session five, read chapters 8–10 of *Your Comeback*.

THE POWER OF GOD'S PRESENCE

We must include God in the thoughts and plans of life, and especially related to a comeback, because He knows what we don't know. He sees every factor, takes into consideration all possibilities, and gives us the best option.

Your Comeback, page 173

Video Teaching Notes

As you watch the video, use the space below to take notes. Some key points and quotes are provided here as reminders.

Tim's Story

In high school, Tim looked to others for his value. His fruitless search for worth led him to alcohol and drug addiction. While under the influence, he had a car accident that left him paralyzed from the waist down. Through all of it, Tim has come to recognize God's presence with him every step of the way. Now he uses his story to influence others in a positive way for the glory of Christ.

No matter where you find yourself today, God is present. When we have to accept that by faith because we can't feel His presence, we need to practice patience and trust in God's sovereignty over our circumstances.

Teaching 1: Tony Evans

1. We have seen that God reigns as sovereign over our circumstances. He is not surprised when we experience trials, and He has a purpose in the midst of them.

2. As we experience difficult times, we need to choose to pursue patience and accept God's direction.

Quotables

- We lean on God's infinite knowledge—first, because our knowledge is limited, and second, because our days are limited.
- You can't change yesterday, but today doesn't have to look like yesterday if you plan in dependence on God's perfect knowledge.
- Submission to God involves a conscious decision to throw back the covers of a lesser, temporary comfort and seek the greater blessing of intimacy with God. Through that, you will find the ability to come back.
- The closer you draw to God, the more like Him you are going to become.

Derek's Story

Derek grew up without a father, an absence that created deep anger and bitterness in him that he released through violence and drug addiction. After years in this lifestyle, he received biblical counseling from the Union Gospel Mission in Spokane, Washington, and surrendered his life to Christ. Since then, he has become the head chef at the mission, where he uses his gifts to minister to other men and share with them the good news of Jesus Christ.

For years, Derek pursued a life on the streets, always looking for that next high. But then God showed him that his real problem was a father wound. Not only was he missing his earthly father, but he also lacked a relationship with his heavenly Father. God used his circumstances to draw Derek to Himself.

Teaching 2: Tony Evans

1. When we find ourselves in trials, we tend to look for a way out. We often praise God for His goodness only after we're on the other side.

2. But God has a purpose for us in our suffering.

3. He is deepening our character, which means we can praise Him in the midst of trials and trust His presence with us.

4. Pursue greater intimacy with God.

Video Group Discussion

1. In the videos, we met two men who sought to fill the gaps in their hearts with substances. As a result, they faced consequences that caused them to struggle even more.

   a. Alcohol and drugs are just two of the things people use to try to fill the gaps in their lives. Some people turn to more socially acceptable alternatives to deal with their pain, disappointment, or unmet needs. What are some of these less offensive tactics?

b. Do you rely on something other than God to ease the pain in your soul? If so, what? Are you willing to let go of it and ask God to fill you instead?

c. Less dangerous dependencies may appear to be safer, but they cost precious time, attention, presence, and spiritual maturity. As a result, they can block you from experiencing your comeback. What are some ways you can overcome other dependencies and transfer your total dependence to God?

2. Derek suffered from a "father wound." This occurs when the role of father is not carried out in a healthy way in the life of a child. What are some other common wounds we may be dealing with that can arise in childhood, teen years, or adulthood?

a. Why is it critical to examine and address these wounds of our souls?

b. In what way does an unaddressed wound lead to bitterness, cynicism, and doubt?

c. How does an understanding of God's sovereignty help to transform and heal the wounds in our lives?

3. In the video, Dr. Evans said there are two ways to face a struggle or challenge: You can remain in it, coping in the misery, or you can look to God to revitalize and heal you so you can rise above it. What are three practical steps you can take to look to God to revitalize and heal you so you can rise above a personal pain, loss, or struggle?

1.

2.

3.

4. Dr. Evans explained in the video that being patient does not mean being passive. We are to be active in overcoming life's challenges or looking for our comeback. He taught us that biblical patience means not going outside of God's authority and provision, trying our own methods to fix what we are facing.

   a. In your own words, describe the difference between pursuing a solution outside of God's will and pursuing a solution within the "ring of obedience."

   b. Can you list a biblical example of someone who went outside God's rule to solve a problem in their life? What was the result?

   c. Does "waiting on God" mean not doing anything? Why or why not?

5. Isaiah 40 tells us that if we are waiting on God and staying within His ring of obedience, but we run out of strength, He will renew our strength.

   a. Have you ever had an experience like that? If so, describe it.

   b. What is true about God's strength that is not true about our own?

Group Bible Exploration

Read Together

You too be patient; strengthen your hearts, for the coming of the Lord is near (James 5:8).

1. What does James mean by "strengthen your hearts"?

2. What are some practical things you can do to strengthen your heart?

Read Together

Come now, you who say, "Today or tomorrow we will go to such and such a city, and spend a year there and engage in business and make a profit." Yet you do not know what your life will be like tomorrow. You are just a vapor that appears for a little while and then vanishes away. Instead, you ought to say, "If the Lord wills, we will live and also do this or that." But as it is, you boast in your arrogance; all such boasting is evil. Therefore, to one who knows the right thing to do and does not do it, to him it is sin (James 4:13-17).

1. What mindset are we expressing when we say, "If the Lord wills"?

2. What are some practical ways we can follow the wisdom of James 4:13-17?

3. The passage in James includes a unique definition of sin. Also read these verses:

This was the guilt of your sister Sodom: she and her daughters had arrogance, abundant food and careless ease, but she did not help the poor and needy (Ezekiel 16:49).

He who shuts his ear to the cry of the poor
Will also cry himself and not be answered (Proverbs 21:13).

a. Based on the principles found in all three passages, why is it important to help those in need?

b. How does refusing to help those in need negatively impact your own life?

c. When you make your plans, do you think about helping those in need? Why or why not? If you do, what are some ways you do this?

Read Together

We are sojourners before You, and tenants, as all our fathers were; our days on the earth are like a shadow, and there is no hope (1 Chronicles 29:15).

My days are swifter than a weaver's shuttle,
And come to an end without hope (Job 7:6).

Teach us to number our days,
That we may present to You a heart of wisdom (Psalm 90:12).

1. What theme do these three verses share?

2. Why is it important to live intentionally in light of the brevity of life?

Read Together

The LORD is near to all who call upon Him,
To all who call upon Him in truth (Psalm 145:18).

You will seek Me and find Me when you search for Me with all your heart (Jeremiah 29:13).

Draw near with confidence (Hebrews 4:16).

Draw near with a sincere heart (Hebrews 10:22).

1. Why do you think God wants us to draw near to Him?

2. What does it mean to search for God with *all* your heart?

3. What are some things that cause us to lack confidence in drawing near to God?

Read Together

Submit therefore to God. Resist the devil and he will flee from you (James 4:7).

1. In what ways can you "resist the devil" in your personal life?

2. In what ways do you tend to give the devil an opportunity to twist your thoughts and choices?

In Closing

As you end this study, remember…

1. Pursuing greater intimacy with God is a key to your comeback.

2. Rather than trying to escape your circumstances, seek a deeper relationship with God in the midst of them.

3. Submit to God's authority in your life. He is in control of your circumstances. He is not surprised by them. They serve His purposes.

4. Cast your cares on God.

5. Humble yourself before God.

6. Obey Him even when it doesn't make sense.

7. Live by faith.

Your story has not come to an end. Persevere, keep pursuing God, and trust Him in all things.

On Your Own in the Coming Days

1. In *Your Comeback*, Dr. Evans compares cultivating intimacy with God and cultivating intimacy in marriage. Maintaining an intimate relationship with anyone takes time and intention.

   a. How high on your priority list is cultivating intimacy with the Lord?

   b. What practical steps can you take to deepen your intimacy with God?

2. Self-Analysis: Character

In the book we've looked at many character qualities that will place you on the path to your comeback:

endurance

wisdom

patience

accepting direction

pursuing intimacy with God

To make this very visual, use this circle to create a pie chart. How big a "slice" of your character is already comprised of each of these qualities?

3. As you look at your completed chart, what can you do to increase the character qualities that are the smallest on your chart?

4. Dr. Evans touches on the concept of timing throughout the book and study. We read, "A lot of us don't get our comeback when we want it simply because it is not yet the right time. We have not yet matured or developed enough to be able to handle it well" (pages 64–65).

   a. In what ways do you still need to mature or develop so you can best be prepared for the comeback you desire?

   b. What steps can you implement to further your spiritual development?

5. Read 2 Corinthians 12:7-9:

   > Because of the surpassing greatness of the revelations, for this reason, to keep me from exalting myself, there was given me a thorn in the flesh, a messenger of Satan to torment me—to keep me from exalting myself! Concerning this I implored the Lord three times that it might leave me. And He has said to me, "My grace is sufficient for you, for power is perfected in weakness." Most gladly, therefore, I will rather boast about my weaknesses, so that the power of Christ may dwell in me.

   a. What was the reason for Paul's "thorn in the flesh"?

   b. Why is it important to maintain a spirit of humility as you pursue your comeback?

   c. In what ways is power perfected in weakness?

   d. Do you have a "thorn in the flesh"? Are you willing to surrender it to God by embracing God's work in and through you and by thanking Him for it?

6. Confession

Take some time before God to confess sins of the heart, such as bitterness, regret, unforgiveness, or doubt. Let Him know that you are willing to surrender these sins under the cross of Jesus Christ and want them replaced with faith, love, grace, and His strength.

After confessing, thank God for His complete forgiveness. Ask Him to usher in your comeback, guiding you along the path He is establishing for you. Thank Him in advance for what He is going to do in your life. Ask Him to bring Himself glory in what He does and to advance His kingdom through you.

DR. TONY EVANS AND THE URBAN ALTERNATIVE

The Urban Alternative (TUA) equips, empowers, and unites Christians to impact individuals, families, churches, and communities through a thoroughly kingdom-agenda worldview. In teaching truth, we seek to transform lives.

The core cause of the problems we face in our personal lives, homes, churches, and societies is a spiritual one. Therefore, the only way to address that core cause is spiritually. We've tried a political, social, economic, and even a religious agenda, and now it's time for a kingdom agenda.

The kingdom agenda can be defined as the visible manifestation of
the comprehensive rule of God over every area of life.

The unifying central theme throughout the Bible is the glory of God and the advancement of His kingdom. The conjoining thread from Genesis to Revelation—from beginning to end—is focused on one thing: God's glory through advancing God's kingdom.

When we do not recognize that theme, the Bible becomes for us a series of disconnected stories that are great for inspiration but seem to be unrelated in purpose and direction. Understanding the role of the kingdom in Scripture increases our understanding of the relevancy of this several-thousand-year-old text to our day-to-day living. That's because God's kingdom was not only then; it is now.

The absence of the kingdom's influence in our personal lives, family lives, churches, and communities has led to a deterioration in our world of immense proportions:

- People live segmented, compartmentalized lives because they lack God's kingdom worldview.

- Families disintegrate because they exist for their own satisfaction rather than for the kingdom.

- Churches are limited in the scope of their impact because they fail to comprehend that the goal of the church is not the church itself but the kingdom.

- Communities have nowhere to turn to find real solutions for real people who have real problems because the church has become divided, in-grown, and unable to transform the cultural and political landscape in any relevant way.

By optimizing the solutions of heaven, the kingdom agenda offers us a way to see and live life with a solid hope. When God is no longer the final and authoritative standard under which all else falls, order and hope have left with Him. But the reverse of that is true as well: as long as we have God, we have hope. If God is still in the picture, and as long as His agenda is still on the table, it's not over.

Even if relationships collapse, God will sustain us. Even if finances dwindle, God will keep us. Even if dreams die, God will revive us. As long as God and His rule are still the overarching standard in our lives, families, churches, and communities, there is always hope.

Our world needs the King's agenda. Our churches need the King's agenda. Our families need the King's agenda.

We've put together a three-part plan to direct us to heal the divisions and strive for unity as we move toward the goal of truly being one nation under God. This three-part plan calls us to assemble with others in unity, to address the issues that divide us, and to act together for social impact. Following this plan, we will see individuals, families, churches, and communities transformed as we follow God's kingdom agenda in every area of our lives. You can request this plan by emailing Info@TonyEvans.org or by going online to TonyEvans.org.

In many major cities, drivers can take a loop to the other side of the city when they don't want to head straight through downtown. This loop takes them close enough to the city center so they can see its towering buildings and skyline but not close enough to actually experience it.

This is precisely what we, as a culture, have done with God. We have put Him on the "loop" of our personal, family, church, and community lives. He's close enough to be at hand should we need Him in an emergency but far enough away that He can't be the center of who we are. We want God on the "loop," not the King of the Bible who comes downtown into the very heart of our ways. And as we have seen in our own lives and in the lives of others, leaving God on the "loop" brings about dire consequences.

But when we make God, and His rule, the centerpiece of all we think, do, or say, we experience Him in the way He longs for us to experience Him. He wants us to be kingdom people with kingdom minds set on fulfilling His kingdom's purposes. He wants us to pray, as Jesus did, "Not my will, but Thy will be done" because His is the kingdom, the power, and the glory.

There is only one God, and we are not Him. As King and Creator, God calls the shots. Only when we align ourselves under His comprehensive hand will we access His full power and authority in all spheres of life: personal, familial, ecclesiastical, and governmental.

As we learn how to govern ourselves under God, we then transform the institutions of family, church, and society using a biblically based kingdom worldview.

Under Him, we touch heaven and change earth.

To achieve our goal, we use a variety of strategies, approaches, and resources for reaching and equipping as many people as possible.

Broadcast Media

Millions of individuals experience *The Alternative with Dr. Tony Evans*, a daily broadcast on nearly 1,400 radio outlets and in more than 130 countries. The broadcast can also be seen on several television networks and is available online at TonyEvans.org. As well, you can listen to or view the daily broadcast by downloading the Tony Evans app for free in the App Store. Over 30,000,000 message downloads/streams occur each year.

Leadership Training

The Tony Evans Training Center (TETC) facilitates a comprehensive discipleship platform, which provides an educational program that embodies the ministry philosophy of Dr. Tony Evans as expressed through the kingdom agenda. The training courses focus on leadership development and discipleship in the following five tracks:

1. Bible & Theology
2. Personal Growth
3. Family and Relationships
4. Church Health and Leadership Development
5. Society and Community Impact Strategies

The TETC program includes courses for both local and online students. Furthermore, TETC programming includes course work for non-student attendees. Pastors, Christian leaders, and Christian laity—both local and at a distance—can seek out the Kingdom Agenda

Certificate for personal, spiritual, and professional development. For more information, visit TonyEvansTraining.org

Kingdom Agenda Pastors (KAP) provides a viable network for like-minded pastors who embrace the kingdom agenda philosophy. Pastors have the opportunity to go deeper with Dr. Tony Evans as they are given greater biblical knowledge, practical applications, and resources to impact individuals, families, churches, and communities. KAP welcomes senior and associate pastors of all churches. KAP also offers an annual Summit held each year in Dallas with intensive seminars, workshops, and resources. For more information, visit KAFellowship.org

Pastors' Wives Ministry, founded by the late Dr. Lois Evans, provides counsel, encouragement, and spiritual resources for pastors' wives as they serve with their husbands in the ministry. A primary focus of the ministry is the KAP Summit, where senior pastors' wives have a safe place to reflect, renew, and relax along with receiving training in personal development, spiritual growth, and care for their emotional and physical well-being. For more information, visit LoisEvans.org.

Kingdom Community Impact

The outreach programs of The Urban Alternative seek to provide positive impact on individuals, churches, families, and communities through a variety of ministries. We see these efforts as necessary to our calling as a ministry and essential to the communities we serve. With training on how to initiate and maintain programs to adopt schools, provide homeless services, and partner toward unity and justice with the local police precincts, which creates a connection between the police and our community, we, as a ministry, live out God's kingdom agenda according to our *Kingdom Strategy for Community Transformation.*

The *Kingdom Strategy for Community Transformation* is a three-part plan that equips churches to have a positive impact on their communities for the kingdom of God. It also provides numerous practical suggestions for how this three-part plan can be implemented in your community, and it serves as a blueprint for unifying churches around the common goal of creating a better world for all of us. For more information, visit TonyEvans.org, then click on the link to access the 3-Point Plan. A course for this strategy is also offered online through the Tony Evans Training Center.

Tony Evans Films ushers in positive life change through compelling video-shorts, animation, and feature-length films. We seek to build kingdom disciples through the power of story. We use a variety of platforms for viewer consumption and have 120,000,000+ digital views. We also merge video-shorts and film with relevant Bible study materials to bring people to the saving knowledge of Jesus Christ and to strengthen the body of Christ worldwide. Tony Evans Films released its first feature-length film, *Kingdom Men Rising*, in April 2019 in more than 800 theaters nationwide in partnership with Lifeway Films. The second release, *Journey with Jesus*, is in partnership with RightNow Media and was released in theaters in November 2021.

Resource Development

By providing a variety of published materials, we are fostering lifelong learning partnerships with the people we serve. Dr. Evans has published more than 125 unique titles based on more than 50 years of preaching—in booklet, book, or Bible study format. He also holds the honor of writing and publishing the first full-Bible commentary and study Bible by an African American, released in 2019. This Bible sits in permanent display as a historic release in the Museum of the Bible in Washington, DC.

For more information and a complimentary copy of Dr. Evans's devotional newsletter, call (800) 800-3222 or write to TUA at P.O. Box 4000, Dallas TX 75208, or visit us online at:

www.TonyEvans.org

MORE GREAT HARVEST HOUSE BOOKS
BY DR. TONY EVANS

30 Days to Overcoming Addictive Behavior

What if, in the next month, you could break the hold a bad habit has on you? Join Dr. Tony Evans on a 30-day journey filled with powerful biblical insights and practical tips for embracing healing and finding liberation.

30 Days to Overcoming Emotional Strongholds

Dr. Evans identifies the most common and problematic emotional strongholds and demonstrates how you can break free from them—by aligning your thoughts with God's truth in the Bible.

30 Days to Victory Through Forgiveness

Has someone betrayed you? Are you suffering the consequences of your own poor choices? Or do you find yourself asking God, "Why did You let this happen?" Like a skilled physician, Dr. Tony Evans leads you through a step-by-step remedy that will bring healing to that festering wound and get you back on your journey to your personal destiny.

Watch Your Mouth

Your greatest enemy is actually in your mouth. Dr. Evans reveals life-changing, biblical insights into the power of the tongue and how your words can be used to bless others or to usher in death. Be challenged to use your mouth to speak life into the world around you. (Also available—*Watch Your Mouth Growth and Study Guide, Watch Your Mouth DVD,* and *Watch Your Mouth Interactive Workbook.*)

It's Not Too Late

Dr. Evans uses prominent Bible characters to show that God delights in using imperfect people who have failed, sinned, or just plain blown it. You'll be encouraged as you come to understand that God has you too on a path to success *despite* your imperfections and mistakes.

The Power of God's Names

Dr. Evans shows that through the names of God, the nature of God is revealed. By understanding the characteristics of God as revealed through His names, you will be better equipped to face the challenges life throws at you.

Praying Through the Names of God

Dr. Evans reveals insights into some of God's powerful names and provides prayers based on those names. Your prayer life will be revitalized as you connect your needs with the relevant characteristics of His names.

Experience the Power of God's Names

Transform your daily life as you learn about the many names of God and the powerful promises they contain. With 85 beautifully designed devotions, this book makes an ideal gift or a great addition to your own quiet time with God.

Victory in Spiritual Warfare

Dr. Evans demystifies spiritual warfare and empowers you with a life-changing truth: Every struggle faced in the physical realm has its root in the spiritual realm. With passion and practicality, Dr. Evans shows you how to live a transformed life in and through the power of Christ's victory.

Prayers for Victory in Spiritual Warfare

Feel defeated? God has given you powerful weapons to help you withstand the onslaught of Satan's lies. This book of prayers, based on Dr. Evans's life-changing book *Victory in Spiritual Warfare*, will help you stand against the enemy's attacks.

To learn more about Harvest House books and
to read sample chapters, visit our website:

www.HarvestHousePublishers.com

HARVEST HOUSE PUBLISHERS
EUGENE, OREGON